English
Pubs

English Pubs

Photographs by Derry Brabbs

WEIDENFELD AND NICOLSON
LONDON

INTRODUCTION

*A*t the heart of every English village, across the green from the church, stands the pub. Witness to the changing fortunes of the area it serves, the local pub is a natural forum for the exchange of gossip, ideas and news, and a resting place for weary travellers.

Pubs and inns reflect the character of their surrounding areas, so there is thatch in the West Country, half-timbering in Hereford and Worcester, brick and flint in the Chilterns and mellow stone in the Cotswolds. Inside, the best of them boast wide open fireplaces, beamed ceilings, cosy snuggeries, and (with luck) well-brewed ale. The landlord may regale customers with tales of the ghosts, smug-

glers and royalty that make up the pub's history, but he will also listen patiently to the story of the one that got away. If talk has no appeal, there's a long tradition of pub games to uphold: skittles, darts, shove ha'penny and dominoes, and usually a willing companion to compete with.

The traditional pub is a haven, whether from ploughing the fields, digging the garden, shiftwork in a factory, a dull day at the office, an empty house or even a leisurely stroll along the local footpaths. From the waterside inn where ducks and swans provide a welcome distraction and boats bob next to the landing stage, via pretty inns with roses framing the door, to the remote moorland pubs of Devon and Yorkshire – a blessing to travellers with many miles behind them and many more ahead – the English pub is an institution that is envied and venerated the world over. To an outsider, its mysteries may be impenetrable and its qualities indefinable, but no community is complete without its local pub.

THE TROUT

*O*N a thirteenth-century site that was once occupied by an Augustinian hospital is a lovely stone building that has been an inn since 1472. Idyllically situated where the River Leach joins the Thames, the pub still has ancient fishing rights to a stretch of the river.

The Bell

*S*TILTON cheeses were sold until 1964 at this former coaching inn in the Cambridgeshire village of the same name – although, curiously, the cheese was never made here. The pub was built in 1515 and is said to have hidden the famous highwayman Dick Turpin for nine weeks.

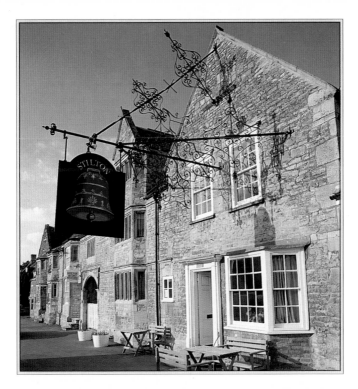

THE GEORGE INN

*T*HIS Hampshire pub displays a number of
interesting architectural features: alternate
courses of brick and flint are set within the
timber work on the ground floor, while,
above, the tiled roof curves gracefully over the
dormer windows.

THE FEATHERS

*W*ELL known to people throughout the region, this attractive mid-sixteenth-century pub in Ledbury, a bustling little town in Hereford and Worcester, is enlivened by its closely knit half-timbered façade.

———◆———

CASTLE INN

*W*ATCHING over this pink-painted Tudor
pub is the twelfth-century Norman keep of
Lydford Castle in Devon. Now a small village,
Lydford was in Saxon times an important town
that boasted a mint.

WHITE SWAN

*L*IKE the cliff-top Barnard Castle opposite,
this fortified stone pub in County Durham
needs to protect itself. Instead of warding off
invaders, however, its stout walls keep out the
rising tide of the River Tees.

ANCHOR INN

*N*EAR the Dorset Coastal Path in Seatown, this seaside pub lies at the foot of the Golden Cap and is a favourite of walkers enjoying some of the most rugged scenery in England.

SMITH'S ARMS

*T*HIS one-room thatched pub, purportedly England's smallest inn, was granted a charter by Charles II. Located in Godmanstone, Dorset, the building dates back to the fifteenth century.

TAN HILL INN

*M*ORE than 1700 feet above sea level, England's highest pub is set in the rugged Yorkshire Dales and offers welcome shelter to walkers of the Pennine Way. Completely isolated, the pub is often cut off by snow in wintertime.

THE MERMAID

*O*VERLOOKING the salt marshes in East Sussex, the town of Rye is filled with attractive buildings dating from the fifteenth to the eighteenth centuries, including this appealing pub on a cobbled street that has remained mostly unaltered since the sixteenth century.

THE RED LION

*S*ITUATED in Avebury, Wiltshire, this lovely half-timbered thatched pub looks out directly onto ancient megaliths that are even older than nearby Stonehenge. The concrete obelisks represent the assumed positions of missing stones.

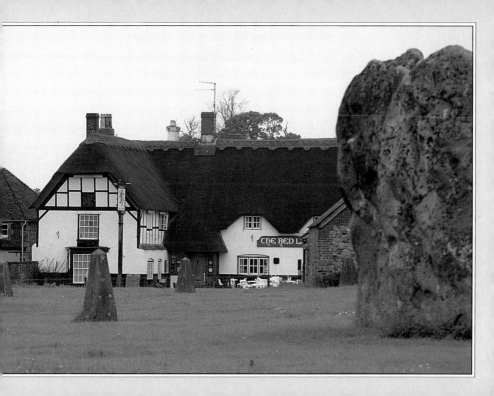

NEW INN

*T*HE high street – appropriately named
Steep Street – of Clovelly, one of Cornwall's
most precipitously charming villages, plunges
down into the sea. At the top of the cobbled
street is a white-painted stone inn that offers
an ideal place to relax after the climb back
up the hill.

THE ROYAL OAK

*S*EA-BIRDS are now the main attraction of this waterside pub in Langstone, Hampshire. The town's name is associated with a group of smugglers who in the eighteenth century made use of the high tides to land their contraband here.

THE SWAN INN

*C*OMPLETELY covered in creeper, this delightful inn in the Cotswold village of Southrop dates back to the mid-seventeenth century. Visitors in spring can also enjoy the village's stunning display of daffodils.

JAMAICA INN

$\mathcal{I}$N the difficult road across Bodmin Moor to west Cornwall, travellers – and at one time smugglers – can seek refuge in the comfort of the grey stone-and-slate pub in Bolventer that was made famous by Daphne du Maurier's eponymous novel.

THE FALKLAND ARMS

*T*HE Oxfordshire village of Great Tew, which has a number of prepossessing buildings and cottages, was home to Viscount Falkland. He surrounded himself with a number of well-known literary figures in the seventeenth century.

THE PANDORA INN

*T*HE waterfront setting of this thatched pub in Cornwall is just one reason for its popularity. Dating back to the fouteenth century, the pub is located on Restronguet Creek, making it vulnerable to the occasional high tide.

THE FEATHERS

*B*UILT in 1603 and featuring the most impressively decorated timber façade in the town, this pub occupies a prominent position in a once prominent locality. The former importance of Ludlow, which sits strategically atop a hill above the rivers Teme and Corve in Shropshire, can be seen in its ruined castle.

❖

WARREN HOUSE

*T*HIS remote pub, which lies on the road that leads through the barren Dartmoor landscape to the prison in Princetown. Built in 1845 for the area's tin-miners, the pub remains a popular gathering place despite the disappearance of the local industry.

HOOPS INN

*L*IKE many of the pubs in Dorset, this inn was once frequented by smugglers. Inside this thatched building in Horns Cross, a resting place for travellers since the thirteenth century, is an ancient well, the water of which was used for brewing ale.

LORD CREWE ARMS

*D*ATING from the thirteenth century, this pub once served the monastic community of Blanchland, deep in the isolated Derwent valley in Northumberland. Long a welcome retreat from the inhospitable moorland in which it lies, the pub is part of the ancient abbey and claims a resident ghost.

THE SWAN

*E*NCLOSED by spectacular scenery, Grasmere was made famous by William Wordsworth, who lived in Dove Cottage from 1799 to 1808. He mentioned this pub in his poem 'The Waggoner'.

THE HORSESHOE

*I*N Shropshire, close to the Welsh border in a village called Llanyblodwel, this charming black-and-white pub perched above the River Tanat dates back to medieval times. As its exterior suggests, the interior contains several rambling low-ceilinged rooms.

THE OLD INN

*T*HIS stone pub dating from the fouteenth century lies in the middle of Dartmoor, in tiny Widecome-in-the-Moor. The village has become popular throughout the country for its annual fair, which takes place in September.

ACKNOWLEDGEMENTS

First published in Great Britain in 1994 by George Weidenfeld and Nicolson Ltd
Orion House, 5 Upper St Martin's Lane, London WC2H 9EA

British Library Cataloguing-in-Publication Data
A catalogue record for this book is available from the British Library

Cover and series design by Peter Bridgewater/Bridgewater Book Company
Series Editor: Lucas Dietrich

*Some of the material in this book was drawn from, among other sources, the Country Series
volume* English Country Pubs *by Derry Brabbs.*